SUPER
FOODS
EVERY DAY

Sue Quinn

SUPER FOODS EVERY DAY

RECIPES USING KALE, BLUEBERRIES,
CHIA SEEDS, CACAO, AND OTHER INGREDIENTS
THAT PROMOTE WHOLE-BODY HEALTH

TEN SPEED PRESS
Berkeley

CONTENTS

WHAT IS A SUPER FOOD?

Super food is a term often exploited by food manufacturers to make products seem more nutritious than they actually are. Sometimes these products lack the scientific evidence to support their alleged health benefits and are no more than fads. This is a shame. Marketing hype aside, there is hard scientific research to show that some foods contain exceptional levels of nutrients that promote good health and protect the human body against disease. These are the super foods I have focused on in this book.

Finding a standard measure of what constitutes a super food is, however, complicated. A number of rating systems have been developed around the world that rank foods according to their nutrient density—the measure of nutrients per calorie. The problem is that these systems are not consistent. For example, some use different sets of essential nutrients as the basis for the rating. What's more, nutrient density is not the only important factor. For example, there are thousands of phytochemicals that appear to have the potential to protect against a range of diseases, but these are not included in nutrient density measures because they have not been established as essential for bodily function.

After researching various rating systems, I have devised my own list of powerhouse foods (see pages 10 to 16) that contain exceptionally high levels of vitamins, phytochemicals, and other nutrients that are strongly associated with good health and reduced risk of chronic disease. The super foods that appear on this list are set in boldface in each recipe's ingredients list so that they can be identified easily. Some ingredients found in the recipes—such as nut milks, wakame, tahini, and miso—are also set in boldface because they are forms of super foods.

The list is by no means exhaustive, but provides a cross-section of super foods in different food groups to help you load your diet with as much goodness as possible.

SUPER FOODS 101

ANTIOXIDANTS

Fruits, vegetables, and grains are the richest sources.

Chemicals that block the activity of **free radicals**.

Protect cells from damage.

CAROTENOIDS

Carotenoids give carrots, squash, and other fruits and vegetables their orange color.

A group of **phytochemicals** that includes carotene, beta-carotene, and lycopene.

Powerful antioxidants.

FLAVONOIDS

Found in berries, tree fruits, nuts, beans, and vegetables, among others.

A large group of **phytochemicals**.

Linked to longevity and reduced risk of heart disease. Powerful antioxidants.

FOLATE

Particularly high levels in dark green leafy vegetables.

A type of **vitamin B**, also known as **folic acid**.

Vital for growth.

FREE RADICALS

Formed naturally in the body, also in the environment: for example cigarette smoke and pollution.

Reactive chemicals that have the potential to damage cells.

Can lead to age-related conditions like cancer, diabetes, and heart disease.

Knowing the common nutritional terms listed here will make it easier to understand the benefits of super foods.

GLUCOSINOLATES

Found in cruciferous vegetables like arugula, bok choy, cabbage, kale, and watercress.

Sulfur-containing chemicals.

Thought to inhibit the development of some cancers.

LYCOPENES

Found in fruits and vegetables such as tomatoes and pink grapefruit.

A group of **phytochemicals** that belong to the family of **carotenoids**.

Powerful antioxidants.

PHYTOCHEMICALS

Nonessential plant-based nutrients with disease protective and preventative properties.

Certain types referred to as **antioxidants, flavonoids, carotenoids,** and **polyphenols.**

May protect against cancer; also linked to lower blood pressure, improved vision, and lower cholesterol.

VITAMIN A

A broad group of nutrients that includes retinoids (from animals) and carotenoids (from plants).

In this book, vitamin A refers to all the combined forms contained in a food.

May protect against cancer; also works as an anti-inflammatory.

VITAMIN C

One of the best-known antioxidants.

VITAMIN E

A generic term for a family of nutrients with powerful antioxidant benefits.

VITAMIN K

Well known for its role in helping blood to clot; also promotes bone strengthening.

SUPER FOODS GLOSSARY

The following list of super foods is drawn from sources including the ANDI (Aggregate Nutrient Density Index) system, the U.S. Centers for Disease Control and Prevention's index of fruits and vegetables ranked by nutrient density[1], and the 100 richest dietary sources of antioxidants as published in the *European Journal of Clinical Nutrition*[2]. Some additional foods identified as having particular health benefits are included. These foods are listed in no particular order.

GREEN VEGETABLES	KEY NUTRIENTS AND POTENTIAL HEALTH BENEFITS
mustard greens	**Vitamins K, A, and C** Lowers cholesterol; cancer protection
turnip greens	**Vitamins K, A, C, and folate, calcium, flavonoids** Protects against cancer and cardiovascular problems; anti-inflammatory
collard greens	**Vitamins K, A, and C, manganese** Protects against cancer and cardiovascular problems; lowers cholesterol; anti-inflammatory
beet greens	**Vitamins K, A, and C, calcium, magnesium** Eye health; comprehensive nourishment

KEY NUTRIENTS AND POTENTIAL HEALTH BENEFITS	GREEN VEGETABLES	
Vitamins K, C, and A Protects against cancer, osteoporosis, and Alzheimer's disease	watercress	
Vitamins K, A, and C, manganese, glucosinolates, flavonoids Lowers cholesterol; cancer protection; anti-inflammatory	kale	
Vitamins K, A, and C, magnesium, flavonoids Anti-inflammatory; regulates blood sugar; cancer protection; supports bone health	Swiss chard	
Vitamins K, C, and A, potassium, glucosinolates Cancer protection; anti-inflammatory	bok choy	
Vitamins K, C, and B6, glucosinolates Cancer protection; anti-inflammatory; lowers cholesterol	cabbage	
Vitamins K and A, folate, manganese, carotenoids Protects against cancer, anti-inflammatory; supports bone health	spinach	
Vitamins K, A, and C, folate Protects against cancer; supports digestive health; lowers cholesterol	Belgian endive	
Vitamins K, A, and C, folate, carotenoids Cancer protection	arugula	
Vitamins K and A, folate, flavonoids, carotenoids Protects against cardiovascular problems; lowers cholesterol	romaine lettuce	

OTHER VEGETABLES	KEY NUTRIENTS AND POTENTIAL HEALTH BENEFITS

 radishes

Vitamin C, carotenoids
Protects against cancer; anti-inflammatory; boosts immunity

 turnips

Vitamin C
Protects against cancer; anti-inflammatory; boosts immunity

 artichoke hearts

Vitamins C and K, folate, fiber
Lowers cholesterol; anti-inflammatory; supports digestive health

 carrots

Vitamins A, K, and B7, carotenoids
Protects against cardiovascular disease and cancer; supports eye health

 acorn squash

Vitamins A, C, and B6, fiber, carotenoids
Anti-inflammatory; regulates blood sugar; protects against heart disease and cancer

 red, yellow, and orange bell peppers

Vitamins C, B6, and A, flavonoids, carotenoids
Regulates blood sugar; protects against heart disease and cancer

 cauliflower

Vitamins C and K, folate
Protects against heart disease and cancer; anti-inflammatory; supports digestive health

 rutabaga

Vitamin C, potassium, carotenoids, fiber
Protects against cancer, heart disease, and bone disease; supports digestive health

KEY NUTRIENTS AND POTENTIAL HEALTH BENEFITS

NUTS AND SEEDS

Omega-3 fatty acids, fiber
Protects against cancer and heart disease; lowers cholesterol;
supports digestive health; eases post-menopausal symptoms

flaxseeds

Vitamin E, B group vitamins, manganese, copper,
carotenoids, fiber
Lowers cholesterol; protects against heart disease, cancer,
and infection; promotes healthy skin

pecans

Vitamin C, B group vitamins, copper, manganese, fiber
Protects against heart disease; lowers cholesterol;
supports bone health

chestnuts

Vitamin E, B group vitamins, manganese, copper, fiber
Protects against heart disease and cancer; lowers cholesterol;
promotes healthy skin

hazelnuts

Copper, manganese, calcium
Relief for rheumatoid arthritis; supports vascular, respiratory,
and bone health; protects against cancer and osteoporosis

sesame seeds

Vitamin E, B group vitamins, copper, manganese, selenium
Lowers cholesterol, prevents heart disease, reduces blood
sugar levels

sunflower seeds

B group vitamins, copper, manganese, flavonoids
Protects against heart disease, stroke, cancer, and
Alzheimer's disease

peanuts

Omega-3 fatty acids, manganese, calcium,
phosphorous, fiber
Limited research, but may support cardiovascular health

chia seeds

FRUITS	KEY NUTRIENTS AND POTENTIAL HEALTH BENEFITS

 cranberries

Vitamin C, flavonoids, other phytochemicals, fiber
Protects against urinary tract infection, cardiovascular disease, and cell damage; anti-inflammatory

 blackberries

Vitamins C and K, folate, manganese, flavonoids, fiber
Protects against cancer and premature aging; regulates blood sugar; anti-inflammatory

 strawberries

Vitamin C, manganese, flavonoids, phytochemicals, fiber
Protects against heart disease and cancer; regulates blood sugar; anti-inflammatory

 raspberries

Vitamin C, manganese, flavonoids, phytochemicals, fiber
Protects against cancer; regulates blood sugar; supports weight loss

 blueberries

Vitamins K and C, manganese, flavonoids
Protects against cardiovascular disease, cancer, and memory loss; supports eye health; regulates blood sugar

 pink and red grapefruits, lemons, limes

Vitamin C, lycopene (pink and red grapefruit only), flavonoids
Protects against cancer, rheumatoid arthritis, and cell damage; supports the immune system; anti-inflammatory

oranges

Vitamin C, flavonoids, fiber
Lowers cholesterol; protects against cancer, heart disease, and rheumatoid arthritis; supports immune system

sweet cherries

Vitamins A and C, flavonoids, phytochemicals
Protects against cancer and cardiovascular disease; anti-inflammatory; calms nervous system

 plums

Vitamin C, flavonoids, phytochemicals
Protects against cell damage; regulates blood sugar; supports weight loss; improves iron absorption

Vitamins C and A
Protects against cancer; antiviral; promotes
good circulation

black elderberries

Vitamin C, carotenoids, flavonoids
Protects against cancer, premature aging, and
neurological disease

aronia berries

Vitamin C, B group vitamins, flavonoids, carotenoids
Protects against cardiovascular disease and cancer; supports
bone health; lowers cholesterol; supports weight loss

tomatoes

Vitamins C and B2, selenium, iron, carotenoids, fiber
Limited research but may offer cancer protection and
supports the immune system; anti-inflammatory

goji berries

Vitamin A, flavonoids, and other phytochemicals
Limited research but, like other dark berries, may protect
against cardiovascular disease and support weight loss

açai berries

Molybdenum (essential mineral), folate, fiber
Lowers cholesterol; regulates blood sugar, protects against
heart disease

pinto, kidney, and
red beans; lentils

Protein, iron, magnesium, calcium
Protects against cancer and heart disease; promotes
bone health

tofu, edamame,
and soy milk

maca powder

Vitamin C, B group vitamins, minerals, phytochemicals
Limited research, but said to boost energy and support
hormone balance

 cocoa powder

B group vitamins, minerals, flavonoids
Antidepressant; mild stimulant; reduces risk of stroke
and heart attack; aids weight loss

 mackerel

Vitamin D, B group vitamins, omega-3 fatty acids
Reduces risk of heart disease; lowers cholesterol;
anti-inflammatory; reduces blood pressure

 salmon

Vitamin D, B group vitamins, selenium, omega-3 fatty acids
Protects against cardiovascular disease and cancer; protects
joints and promotes eye health

 seaweed

Vitamin C, iodine, minerals, phytochemicals
Anti-inflammatory; lowers cholesterol; protects
against cancer

 basil

Vitamin K, flavonoids
Regulates blood sugar; lowers cholesterol; antibacterial

 coriander seeds
and cilantro

Vitamin K, flavonoids, other phytochemicals
Regulates blood sugar; lowers cholesterol; antibacterial

[1] Di Noia J., "Defining Powerhouse Fruits and Vegetables: A Nutrient Density Approach," *Preventing Chronic Disease;*
June 11, 2014.
[2] J. Pérez-Jiménez, V. Neveu, F. Vos, and A. Scalbert, "Identification of the 100 richest dietary sources of polyphenols: an
application of the Phenol-Explorer database," *European Journal of Clinical Nutrition* 64, S112–S120; November 2010.

VITAMINS IN SUPER FOODS

Use the information below to identify which super foods are the best sources for key vitamins[3].

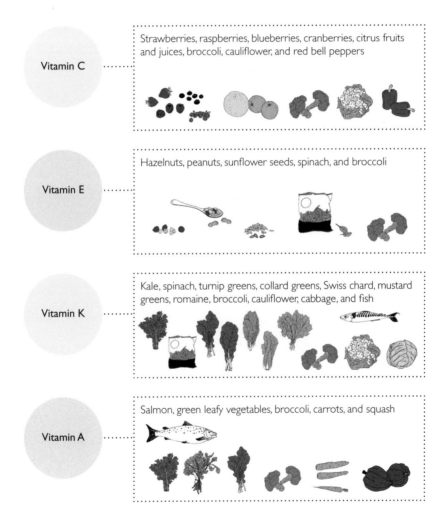

Vitamin C

Strawberries, raspberries, blueberries, cranberries, citrus fruits and juices, broccoli, cauliflower, and red bell peppers

Vitamin E

Hazelnuts, peanuts, sunflower seeds, spinach, and broccoli

Vitamin K

Kale, spinach, turnip greens, collard greens, Swiss chard, mustard greens, romaine, broccoli, cauliflower, cabbage, and fish

Vitamin A

Salmon, green leafy vegetables, broccoli, carrots, and squash

[3] WHFoods.org and the George Mateljan Foundation; U.S. National Institutes of Health.

BREAKFAST

Start the day with one of these powerhouse breakfast ideas. Nutrient-packed smoothies provide a quick shot of goodness for those in a hurry, while bowls and toasts are perfect for fueling up with super seeds, berries, and nuts.

CHOCO SMOOTHIE

Serves: 1 person — Time: 5 minutes

CONTAINS
Vitamins B group, C, and E, minerals, flavonoids,
phytochemicals, omega-3 fatty acids, fiber, protein,
iron, magnesium, manganese, phosphorous,
selenium, copper, and calcium

INGREDIENTS
1 cup milk of choice, such as dairy, **soy**, or **flax**, plus more

1 small banana • 1½ teaspoons **cocoa powder** or **cacao nibs**

1½ teaspoons **maca powder** • 1 teaspoon each **flaxseeds**, **chia seeds**, and

sunflower seeds • 2 tablespoons rolled oats • 1 tablespoon honey or agave nectar

POTENTIAL
BENEFITS
protects against *cancer,
heart disease* • **lowers**
cholesterol, blood sugar levels
• **supports** *weight loss, digestive,
cardiovascular, and bone health,
hormone balance* • **eases**
postmenopausal symptoms
• *antidepressant; mild
stimulant; boosts
energy*

Place all the ingredients in a bender and blend on high speed until
smooth and creamy, adding more milk if needed to achieve the desired
consistency. Taste and add more honey if needed before serving.

WONDER SMOOTHIE

Serves: 1 person — Time: 5 minutes

CONTAINS
Vitamins A, C, and K, folate, manganese,
glucosinolates, flavonoids, carotenoids, and fiber

INGREDIENTS
1 pear, cored and chopped, skin on • 1 apple, cored and chopped, skin on
2 small handfuls of **kale** • 1 small handful of **spinach**
Juice of 1 **lime** • ⅓ cup **orange juice** • ½ teaspoon grated fresh ginger

**POTENTIAL
BENEFITS**

*protects against cancer,
cell damage, heart disease,
rheumatoid arthritis*
• **lowers** *cholesterol*
• **supports** *bone health,
immune system*
• *anti-inflammatory*

Place all the ingredients in a blender and blend on high speed until smooth. Depending on the power of your blender, you might need to push the mixture through a fine-mesh sieve to achieve a smoother consistency.

BERRY BLAST SMOOTHIE

Serves: 1 person — Time: 5 minutes

CONTAINS

Vitamins A, C, and K, folate, manganese, omega-3
fatty acids, flavonoids, phytochemicals, calcium,
phosphorous, protein, iron, magnesium, fiber

INGREDIENTS

⅓ cup **blackberries** • ⅓ cup **blueberries** • ⅓ cup **raspberries**

¼ cup **açai juice** • ¼ teaspoon grated fresh ginger

2 teaspoons **chia seeds** • 1 cup **flax, soy,** or dairy milk

1 tablespoon honey • 1 tablespoon plain yogurt

POTENTIAL
BENEFITS
protects against
*cardiovascular disease, cancer,
memory loss, premature aging*
• **lowers** *cholesterol*
• **supports** *eye, digestive, and bone
health; weight loss* • **regulates**
blood sugar • **eases** *post-
menopausal symptoms*
• *anti inflammatory*

Place all the ingredients in a blender and blend on high speed for
2 minutes, or until combined and the seeds are completely broken
down. Push through a fine-mesh sieve if necessary to achieve the desired
consistency. Taste and add more honey if needed before serving.

STRAWBERRY SUPERSPREAD

Makes: about 1¼ cups — Time: 15 minutes, plus 10 minutes to thicken

CONTAINS

Vitamin C, manganese, flavonoids, phytochemicals,
omega-3 fatty acids, manganese, calcium,
phosphorous, fiber

INGREDIENTS

4 cups (1 pound) **strawberries**, hulled and quartered

2 to 3 tablespoons honey • A squeeze of **lemon**

3 tablespoons **chia seeds**, plus more if needed

POTENTIAL
BENEFITS

protects against *heart disease, cancer, rheumatoid arthritis, cell damage*
• **regulates** *blood sugar*
• **supports** *immune system, cardiovascular health*
• *anti-inflammatory*

Place the strawberries in a saucepan and mash with a potato masher. Cook over medium-low heat, stirring, until the berries release their juice. Stir in the honey and lemon, increase the heat, and simmer for 10 minutes, or until thickened. Remove from the heat and stir in the chia seeds. Set aside for 10 minutes; if the mixture hasn't thickened into a jam, add more chia seeds and/or return to the heat for a few more minutes. Cool, then store in an airtight container in the fridge.

SPICED POWER POT

Serves: 1 person — Time: 1 hour

CONTAINS
Vitamins A, B group, C, and E, fiber, carotenoids,
copper, manganese, selenium

INGREDIENTS

½ **acorn squash** (about 10 ounces), seeded and cut into large chunks with skin on

A generous pinch of cinnamon • A scant pinch of nutmeg

1½ teaspoons unsalted butter • 1 tablespoon rolled oats or spelt flakes

1½ teaspoons **sunflower seeds** • 1½ teaspoons pumpkin seeds

Pinch of fine sea salt • 1½ teaspoons honey • ½ cup Greek yogurt

POTENTIAL
BENEFITS

protects against
cancer, heart disease
• **lowers** *cholesterol*
• **regulates** *blood sugar*
• *anti-inflammatory*

Preheat the oven to 350°F. Roast the squash for 30 to 40 minutes until tender. Cool slightly, then scrape the flesh into a food processor, add the cinnamon and nutmeg and purée. Set aside to cool. Heat the butter in a small frying pan and add the oats, seeds, and salt. Stir-fry over medium-high heat until lightly toasted; don't burn the seeds. Add the honey and stir-fry for 1 minute, until sticky. Cool on a plate, then break into pieces. To serve, layer the yogurt, squash purée, and seeds in a small glass jar or bowl.

CHERRY CRUSH TOASTS

Serves: 1 person — Time: 15 minutes

CONTAINS

Vitamins A, B group, C, E, and K, flavonoids,
phytochemicals, copper, manganese, selenium, calcium,
omega-3 fatty acids, phosphorous, fiber

INGREDIENTS

4 ounces **sweet cherries**, fresh or frozen, pitted • 1 tablespoon honey
or agave nectar • 1 tablespoon **lemon juice** • 2 **basil** leaves
1 or 2 slices **seedy bread** • 2 to 3 tablespoons Greek yogurt
or cream cheese • **Sesame seeds**, for sprinkling

Place the cherries, honey, and lemon juice in a pan and lightly crush with
a potato masher. Bring to a gentle simmer, then reduce the heat to low,
cover and cook for 5 minutes. Tear the basil leaves into the pan and gently
simmer, uncovered, for another 5 minutes, until the juices reduce to a syrup.
Meanwhile, toast the bread and spread with the yogurt. To serve, spoon the
cherries and sauce over the yogurt and sprinkle with sesame seeds.

31

GET-THE-GLOW PORRIDGE

Serves: 1 person — Time: 20 minutes

CONTAINS

Vitamins B group, C, E, and K, manganese, flavonoids,
carotenoids, phytochemicals, copper, selenium,
omega-3 fatty acids, fiber

INGREDIENTS

¼ cup **raspberries** • ¼ cup **blueberries**

1½ cups **flax**, almond, or dairy milk, plus more to serve

2 tablespoons rolled oats • 2 tablespoons quinoa flakes

1 tablespoon **sunflower seeds** • 1 teaspoon **flaxseeds**

Pinch of fine sea salt • ½ teaspoon ground cinnamon

1 tablespoon honey • Chopped **pecans** or **hazelnuts**, to serve

Blend the berries in a food processor or blender then set aside. Gently heat
the milk in a saucepan and keep warm. Combine the oats, quinoa flakes,
and seeds in another saucepan and cook, stirring, over medium-high heat until
the mixture smells nutty and toasted. Add half the warm milk, stir briskly, and then
add the cinnamon and honey. Cook gently for 15 minutes, stirring, and adding
the remaining warm milk, plus extra cold milk if needed, to maintain the desired
consistency. Pour into a bowl, swirl the berry sauce in, and sprinkle with nuts.

SUPER MUESLI

Makes: about 1½ pounds; serves 8 people — Time: 5 minutes

CONTAINS

Vitamins B group, C, and E, manganese, copper,
carotenoids, omega-3 fatty acids, calcium,
phosphorous, fiber, selenium, iron

INGREDIENTS

1¼ cups rolled oats • 1¼ cups quinoa flakes • ⅔ cup **pecans**, coarsely chopped

3 tablespoons **chia seeds** • ½ cup dried mango, coarsely chopped

¼ cup **goji berries** • 2 teaspoons ground cinnamon

Pinch of fine sea salt • ½ cup dried apricots, coarsely chopped

½ cup pumpkin seeds • 2 tablespoons **sesame seeds**

In a large mixing bowl, stir together all the ingredients until evenly distributed.
Store in an airtight container. Serve with yogurt or milk.

SALADS, SOUPS, AND SMALL PLATES

Salads and soups are ideal for squeezing as much goodness into one bowl as possible, and the recipes here are brimming with antioxidants and other nutrients. There are also plates of tasty goodness that you can keep to yourself or share—if you want to.

GO-TO CLEANSE SALAD

Serves: 1 person – Time: 5 minutes

CONTAINS
Vitamins A, B group C, E, and K, manganese, copper,
selenium, flavonoids, fiber

INGREDIENTS

1½ teaspoons chopped **blanched hazelnuts** • 1½ teaspoons **sunflower seeds**

½ teaspoon nigella seeds • A pinch of fine sea salt

2 ounces **watercress** or **upland cress** (weighed without thick stalks)

1 tablespoon **lemon juice** • 3 tablespoons extra-virgin olive oil

For the salad, place the nuts, seeds, and salt in a frying pan over medium heat and toast, stirring, until aromatic. Be careful not to burn. Set aside to cool. Place the watercress in a salad bowl. Gently toss with lemon juice and olive oil and scatter with the seed mixture. Serve immediately.

SUPER SALAD

Serves: 1 person as a main dish — Time: 10 minutes

CONTAINS
Vitamins A, B group, C, E, and K, carotenoids,
manganese, glucosinolates, flavonoids, copper,
selenium, iron, fiber

INGREDIENTS

3 tablespoons extra-virgin olive oil • 1 teaspoon **lemon juice** • 1 teaspoon honey

½ clove garlic, minced • Sea salt flakes • Freshly ground black pepper

4 ounces **kale leaves**, finely sliced • 3 ounces **cabbage**, shredded

1 medium **carrot**, grated • 1 avocado, pitted, peeled, and sliced

3 tablespoons **sunflower seeds** • ⅔ cup **blueberries**

2 tablespoons **goji berries** or **aronia berries**, or a mixture

POTENTIAL
BENEFITS

protects against *cancer,
rheumatoid arthritis, cardiovascular
disease, neurological disease,
memory loss, premature aging and
cell damage* • **lowers** *cholesterol*
• **regulates** *blood sugar levels*
• **supports** *immune
system and eye health*
• *anti-inflammatory*

Whisk together the oil, lemon juice, honey, and garlic, and season
with salt and pepper. Set aside. Place the remaining ingredients in a
salad bowl. Toss with the dressing and serve immediately.

VIBRANT BREAD SALAD

Serves: 4 people as a side — Time: 20 minutes

CONTAINS

Vitamins A, B group, C, and K, copper, manganese,
calcium, glucosinolates, flavonoids, carotenoids

INGREDIENTS

2 pitas • 1 clove garlic, halved

2 tablespoons extra-virgin olive oil, plus more for brushing and drizzling

3 tablespoons **tahini** • 2 tablespoons **lemon juice**

1 teaspoon sumac or smoked sweet paprika • Sea salt flakes

Freshly ground black pepper • A large handful of **baby kale** • 2 ounces **watercress**

2 to 3 small **tomatoes** (about 8 ounces), chopped • 4 ounces **radishes**, chopped

Preheat the oven to 350°F. Rub the pitas on both sides with the cut garlic; reserve the garlic. Brush with olive oil, cut into bite-sized pieces, and place on a baking tray. Bake for 10 minutes, until starting to crisp. To make the dressing, crush the reserved garlic in a screw-top jar and add the 2 tablespoons of oil, tahini, lemon juice, sumac, and ¼ cup of cold water. Season with salt and pepper, shake vigorously, and set aside. Place all the remaining ingredients in a salad bowl, add the toasted pita, and toss with enough of the dressing to coat. Serve immediately.

SESAME CRUNCH BOWL

Serves: 1 person — Time: 15 to 20 minutes

CONTAINS
Vitamins A, C, and K, copper, manganese, calcium, folate,
carotenoids, glucosinolates, flavonoids, potassium

INGREDIENTS

3 tablespoons toasted **sesame oil** • 3 ounces shiitake mushrooms, sliced

1 tablespoon sake • 1½ teaspoons mirin • Sea salt flakes

Freshly ground black pepper • 2 teaspoons rice wine vinegar

1½ teaspoons fish sauce • ½ teaspoon grated fresh ginger

20 ounces mixed greens such as **arugula**, **baby kale**, and **baby mustard leaves**

1 to 2 heads **bok choy** (about 3 ounces), leaves separated and large leaves halved

1 large or a few baby **radishes** (about 2 ounces), finely sliced

Heat 1 tablespoon of the sesame oil in a frying pan and sauté the mushrooms
until they are soft and releasing their juices. Add the sake and mirin and let
the liquid bubble away, then season with salt and pepper. Set aside to cool a
little. Place the remaining sesame oil, the vinegar, fish sauce, ginger, and more
salt and pepper in a screw-top jar and shake to combine. Place the mixed
greens, bok choy, radishes, and cooled mushrooms in a bowl and toss with
enough of the dressing to coat well. Serve immediately.

SUPERSLAW

Serves: 4 people as a side — Time: 30 minutes (10 active)

CONTAINS

Vitamins A, C, K, and B7, copper, manganese, calcium,
flavonoids and other phytochemicals, potassium,
carotenoids, fiber

INGREDIENTS

2 tablespoons plain yogurt • 2 tablespoons **tahini**

1 tablespoon **lemon juice**, plus more • ½ clove garlic, minced

Sea salt flakes • Freshly ground black pepper

½ medium **turnip** (about 4 ounces), peeled and sliced into matchsticks

½ medium **rutabaga** (about 6 ounces), peeled and sliced into matchsticks

1 medium **carrot**, peeled • 1 red apple • 1 small handful **cilantro**, chopped

For the dressing, place the yogurt, tahini, lemon juice, and garlic in a
screw-top jar. Season with salt and pepper, add 2 tablespoons of water, and
shake vigorously to combine. Set aside. For the salad, place the vegetables
and apple in a salad bowl and add the cilantro. Pour over the dressing
and toss to coat. Add more lemon juice, salt, and pepper to taste. Set aside
for up to 20 minutes before serving to let the flavors infuse.

GOODNESS BOWL

Serves: 1 person   —   Time: 20 minutes

CONTAINS
Vitamins A, B group, C, and K, manganese, copper,
glucosinolates, flavonoids and other phytochemicals,
calcium, magnesium

INGREDIENTS
Scant ½ cup red quinoa, rinsed and drained

A large mixed handful of **kale**, **mustard leaves**, and **beet greens**, finely sliced

1 green onion, finely sliced • ½ jalapeño, seeded and finely chopped

1 tablespoon chopped **cilantro** • 2 tablespoons extra virgin olive oil

2 tablespoons **lime juice** • ½ clove garlic, crushed • Sea salt flakes

Freshly ground black pepper • 1 hard-boiled egg, halved

2 tablespoons toasted **peanuts**, coarsely chopped

POTENTIAL
BENEFITS

protects against *cancer,*
rheumatoid arthritis, cell
damage, heart disease, stroke,
and Alzheimer's disease • lowers
cholesterol • regulates *blood*
sugar • supports *eye health*
and the immune system
• *anti-inflammatory,*
antibacterial

Cook the quinoa according to the package instructions. Drain (if necessary) and set aside. Steam the mixed greens until just tender. Place all the remaining ingredients except the peanuts and egg in a screw-top jar and shake to combine. To serve, place the quinoa in a bowl and top with the steamed vegetables and egg. Spoon over the dressing, scatter with the peanuts, and serve immediately.

ZINGY CHEAT'S PIZZA

Serves: 1 person — Time: 15 minutes

CONTAINS
Vitamins A, B group, C, and K, flavonoids, carotenoids,
folate, manganese, fiber

INGREDIENTS

½ (14-ounce) can chopped **tomatoes** • Sea salt flakes
Freshly ground black pepper • 1 large tortilla • A handful of **baby spinach**, sliced
4 **artichoke hearts** in oil, drained and quartered
Peel from ½ **preserved lemon**, finely sliced • 1 mozzarella ball (about 4 ounces), sliced
Extra-virgin olive oil, for drizzling • **Basil** leaves, for sprinkling

Pour the tomatoes into a small saucepan, season with salt and pepper, stir, and simmer over low heat until thickened, about 10 minutes. Set aside. Heat a frying pan. Cook the tortilla in the hot pan until it starts to puff up and turn brown. Transfer to a baking sheet and spread the tomato sauce over the top. Arrange the spinach, artichokes, and preserved lemon peel on top, and season with salt and pepper. Top with the mozzarella slices and drizzle with olive oil. Place under the broiler until the cheese melts and turns golden. Sprinkle with basil leaves, cut into slices, and serve.

TOFU BITES AND PUNCHY PICKLES

Serves: 2 to 4 people as a side — Time: 30 minutes

CONTAINS
Vitamins A, C, K, and B7, carotenoids, flavonoids,
protein, iron, magnesium, and calcium

INGREDIENTS

1 large **carrot**, peeled and cut into fine matchsticks • 1 teaspoon superfine sugar

¼ teaspoon fine sea salt • ¼ cup rice vinegar

1 tablespoon soy sauce • 1½ tablespoons **lime juice**

1½ teaspoons dashi or vegetable stock • ¾ cup cornstarch

Sea salt flakes • Freshly ground black pepper

12 ounces **silken tofu**, cut into ¾-inch squares • Vegetable oil, for frying

POTENTIAL
BENEFITS

protects against
cardiovascular disease,
rheumatoid arthritis,
cell damage, and cancer
• **supports** *eye and bone health*
and immune system
• *anti-inflammatory*

Toss together the carrot, sugar, fine sea salt, and half the vinegar. Set aside for 30 minutes, then drain. Meanwhile, whisk together the remaining vinegar, the soy sauce, lime juice, and dashi in a small bowl and set aside. Place the cornstarch on a shallow plate and season with salt flakes and pepper. Roll the tofu in the cornstarch to coat. Heat enough oil in a frying pan to come ¼ inch up the sides and fry the tofu, turning constantly, for 5 minutes, until crisp and golden all over. Serve immediately, with the pickled carrots and sauce alongside for dipping.

SUNSHINE SOUP

Serves: 4 people — Time: about 50 minutes

CONTAINS

Vitamins A, B group, and C, flavonoids, carotenoids,
copper, manganese, calcium

INGREDIENTS

2 **red**, **yellow**, or **orange bell peppers**, halved and seeded

3 to 4 medium **tomatoes** (about 18 ounces), halved

2 tablespoons extra-virgin olive oil, plus more for drizzling

A pinch of saffron threads, chopped • 1 quart hot chicken or vegetable stock

1 red onion, chopped • 2 cloves garlic, finely sliced

1 heaping teaspoon fresh oregano, chopped • Sea salt flakes

Freshly ground black pepper • Plain yogurt or crème fraîche, to serve

Sesame seeds, toasted, to serve

Place the peppers and tomatoes in a baking tray cut-side down. Drizzle with olive
oil, and place under the broiler until the peppers blacken and the tomatoes
blister. Cool down, then peel off the pepper skins. Add the saffron to the stock
and set aside. Heat the 2 tablespoons of olive oil in a large saucepan and sauté the
onion for 8 minutes until soft. Add the garlic and sauté for a few minutes. Add
the grilled peppers and tomatoes, stock, and oregano. Season with salt and pepper
and simmer for 20 minutes. Cool slightly, then purée in a food processor or with
a hand blender. Warm through. Serve with a swirl of yogurt and sesame seeds.

SOUP SOOTHER

Serves: 4 people — *Time: 20 minutes*

CONTAINS

Vitamins A, C, and K, potassium, glucosinolates,
copper, magnesium, iodine, minerals, phytochemicals,
calcium, protein, iron

INGREDIENTS

2 cups vegetable or chicken stock • 1½ teaspoons soy sauce

1 teaspoon dried **wakame** • 3 ounces firm **tofu**, cubed

1 head of **bok choy** (about 4 ounces), leaves trimmed and separated

Place the stock in a saucepan and add the soy sauce. Bring to a boil, then set aside for 10 minutes. Meanwhile, soak the wakame in hot water for 10 minutes, then drain and cut away any tough spines. Add the wakame, tofu, and bok choy to each of the 4 bowls. Pour the stock into the bowls and serve immediately.

CREAMY COMFORT SOUP

Serves: 4 people — Time: about 30 minutes

CONTAINS
Vitamins C and K, folate, molybdenum, fiber

INGREDIENTS

2 tablespoons olive oil • 1 red onion, chopped • 1 teaspoon ground cumin
10 ounces **cauliflower**, cut into florets and stalks chopped • 1 quart vegetable stock
1½ cups cooked or canned **red kidney** or **pinto beans**, drained and rinsed
Fine sea salt • Freshly ground black pepper • Crème fraîche, to serve

POTENTIAL
BENEFITS

protects against *heart disease and cancer*
• **lowers** *cholesterol*
• **regulates** *blood sugar*
• **supports** *digestive health*
• *anti-inflammatory*

Heat the oil in a large saucepan and cook the onion for about 8 minutes
until soft. Add the cumin and the cauliflower and cook over medium-high
heat, stirring, until the cauliflower starts to brown. Add the stock and beans.
Reduce the heat and simmer, uncovered, until the cauliflower is tender.
When the cauliflower is cooked, cool slightly, then carefully purée the soup in
a food processor or with a hand blender. Warm through over medium heat,
add salt and pepper to taste, and top with crème fraîche before serving.

PEANUT HUMMUS

Serves: 2 to 4 people as a side — Time: 5 minutes

CONTAINS
Vitamins B group and C, copper, manganese, flavonoids

INGREDIENTS
1 (14-ounce) can chickpeas • 1 small clove garlic
3 tablespoons smooth **peanut butter** • 3 tablespoons **lemon juice**, plus more
1½ teaspoons ground cumin • Sea salt flakes • Freshly ground black pepper
Extra-virgin olive oil, for drizzling • Chopped vegetables, to serve

POTENTIAL
BENEFITS

protects against *heart
disease, stroke, cancer,
Alzheimer's disease, rheumatoid
arthritis, and cell damage*
• **supports** *the immune system*
• *anti-inflammatory*

Drain the chickpeas, reserving the liquid, and rinse. Combine the
chickpeas, garlic, peanut butter, lemon juice, and cumin in a food
processor and process until smooth. Add some of the reserved chickpea
liquid to loosen if the purée is too thick, and adjust the seasoning
according to taste with extra lemon juice and salt and pepper. Transfer to
a shallow bowl and drizzle with olive oil. Serve with chopped vegetables.

VITA FRITTATA

Serves: 4 to 6 people – Time: 45 minutes

CONTAINS
Vitamins A, B6, C, and K, carotenoids, magnesium,
flavonoids, molybdenum, folate, fiber

INGREDIENTS
½ **acorn squash** (about 10 ounces), peeled, seeded, and diced small

4 tablespoons olive oil • Sea salt flakes • Freshly ground black pepper

5 ounces **Swiss chard**, sliced • 4 eggs, lightly beaten

1¼ cups cooked **black**, **green**, or **Puy lentils** • 3½ ounces feta cheese, crumbled

Preheat the oven to 400°F. Place the squash on a baking tray, toss with
1 tablespoon of oil and season with salt and pepper. Roast for 30 minutes, or
until tender. Heat 1 tablespoon of oil in an 8-inch frying pan and sauté the
Swiss chard, season with salt and pepper. Transfer to a bowl, leave to cool
slightly, then stir in the eggs, lentils, cheese, and squash. Wipe out the frying
pan, heat the remaining oil, and pour in the egg mixture. Cook over medium-
high heat until golden underneath, about 15 minutes, then place under the
broiler until set, about 5 minutes. Invert onto a plate to serve.

SIDE DISHES

*Just because sides are the supporting role in
a meal doesn't mean they can't be packed with
nutrients. In fact, all these sides are so loaded
with flavor and goodness you could enjoy
them as stand-alone meals. Eating your greens
has never been easier.*

POWER PLATE

Serves: 4 people — Time: 40 minutes

CONTAINS

Vitamins A, B group, C, and K, copper, manganese,
fiber, carotenoids, calcium, magnesium, flavonoids,
other phytochemicals

INGREDIENTS

1 to 2 **acorn squash** (about 1¾ pounds), cut into ¾-inch wedges at the widest part

3 tablespoons olive oil, plus more for drizzling • Sea salt flakes

Freshly ground black pepper • 6 ounces vacuum-packed **chestnuts**, halved

6 tablespoons Greek yogurt • 1 tablespoon sriracha sauce, or more

2 large handfuls of **beet greens**, chopped • 1 large handful of **cilantro**, chopped

POTENTIAL
BENEFITS

protects against *heart
disease and cancer*
• lowers *cholesterol*
• regulates *blood sugar*
• supports *bone and eye health
and comprehensive nourishment*
• *anti-inflammatory,
antibacterial*

Heat the oven to 400°F. Place the squash on a baking tray, toss with the olive oil, and season with salt and pepper. Roast for 30 minutes, until almost tender. Add the chestnuts to the pan, turn to coat in the oil and return to the oven for another 10 minutes. To make the dressing, stir together the yogurt and sriracha. To serve, scatter the beet greens over a serving platter, drizzle with olive oil, and toss to coat. Arrange the roasted squash and chestnuts on top, then pour over the yogurt dressing. Serve scattered with the cilantro.

SPICY STIR-FRIED GREENS

Serves: 4 people — Time: 10 minutes

CONTAINS

Vitamins A, C, and K, flavonoids and other
phytochemicals, potassium, glucosinolates, copper,
manganese, calcium

INGREDIENTS

2 tablespoons peanut or other flavorless oil • 1¼-inch piece fresh ginger, peeled
and finely chopped • A small handful of **cilantro**, finely chopped

1 red chile, such as a Thai chile, seeded and finely sliced

4 large heads of **bok choy**, quartered lengthwise • 2 tablespoons mirin

½ cup chicken or vegetable stock • A splash of soy sauce, or more

Toasted sesame oil, for drizzling

Heat the oil in a frying pan or wok over high heat. Add the ginger, cilantro and chile, and stir-fry for 1 minute. Add the bok choy and cook until starting to soften, then add the mirin, stock, and soy sauce. Cook until the bok choy is tender but still retains some bite, about 5 minutes. Transfer to a serving bowl and drizzle with sesame oil. Serve immediately.

GREEN SMASH

Serves: 4 people — Time: 30 minutes

CONTAINS

Vitamins A, B6, C, and K, manganese, glucosinolates,
flavonoids, omega-3 fatty acids, fiber, protein, iron,
magnesium, and calcium

INGREDIENTS

1⅓ pounds floury potatoes, cut into chunks with the skins left on

2 tablespoons unsalted butter • 2 ounces **kale**, finely sliced • 2 ounces **collard greens**

or **spring greens**, finely sliced • 2 ounces **cabbage**, finely sliced

¾ cup **flax**, **soy**, or dairy milk, plus more if needed

1 clove garlic, bruised • Sea salt flakes • Freshly ground black pepper

Steam the potatoes until tender. Melt half the butter in a large frying pan
and add the kale, collard greens, and cabbage. Stir-fry until tender but retaining
some bite, about 2 minutes. Set aside. Place the milk in a pan with the garlic,
bring to a boil, then remove from the heat and keep warm. When the potatoes
are cooked, mash with the remaining butter and milk (discarding the garlic) until
smooth and creamy. Add more milk if necessary to achieve the desired consistency.
Mix in the vegetables and add salt and pepper to taste. Serve immediately.

NUTTY GRILLED LETTUCE

Serves: 4 people — Time: 15 minutes

CONTAINS
Vitamins A, B group, E, and K, folate, flavonoids,
carotenoids, manganese, copper, fiber

INGREDIENTS

2 tablespoons mayonnaise • 2 tablespoons crème fraîche

½ clove garlic, crushed • 5 **basil** leaves, finely sliced

Sea salt flakes • Freshly ground black pepper

3 large **romaine lettuce hearts**, halved lengthwise • Extra-virgin olive oil, for brushing

3 hard-boiled eggs, chopped • 3 tablespoons **toasted hazelnuts**, chopped

For the dressing, place the mayonnaise, crème fraîche, garlic, basil, and a splash of water in a screw-top jar. Season with salt and pepper and shake vigorously. Add more water to loosen if needed. Set aside. Heat a ridged grill pan over high heat. Brush the cut side of the lettuce with olive oil and grill cut-side down until charred and slightly wilted. Flip and briefly cook the other side—the lettuce should still be firm at the center. Transfer to a serving plate, drizzle with the dressing, and top with the chopped eggs. Drizzle over more dressing and scatter with the hazelnuts to serve.

GLOWING GREENS

Serves: 4 people as a side — Time: 10 minutes

CONTAINS
Vitamins A, B group, C, E, and K, manganese,
glucosinolates, flavonoids, folate, copper, fiber

INGREDIENTS
10 ounces mixed leafy greens such as **collard greens** or **spring greens**,
kale, and **endive**, sliced • 2 tablespoons **hazelnut oil**
¼ cup balsamic vinegar • 5 tablespoons unsalted butter • Sea salt flakes
Freshly ground black pepper

POTENTIAL
BENEFITS

protects against *cancer
and cardiovascular problems*
• **lowers** *cholesterol*
• **supports** *digestive and
skin health*
• *anti-inflammatory*

Steam the leafy greens for about 2 minutes, until just tender. Transfer to
a serving bowl, toss with the hazelnut oil, and set aside somewhere warm.
Place the balsamic vinegar in a small pan and cook over medium heat,
stirring constantly while the mixture bubbles and thickens to a syrup, about
5 minutes. Add the butter and stir until melted. Pour the syrup over the
greens, toss, and season generously with salt and pepper. Serve immediately.

CREAMY TURNIP BAKE

Serves: 4 people — Time: 50 minutes

CONTAINS

Vitamins A, C, and K, folate, calcium, flavonoids,
omega-3 fatty acids, fiber, protein, iron, magnesium,
carotenoids, manganese, glucosinolates

INGREDIENTS

1⅔ cups **flax**, **soy**, or dairy milk, plus more if needed • 1⅔ cups heavy cream

2 cloves garlic, minced • 2 thyme sprigs

2 bay leaves • Sea salt flakes • Freshly ground black pepper

3 to 4 medium **turnips** (about 1⅓ pounds), peeled and finely sliced

(ideally on a mandoline) • A large handful of **turnip greens** (**baby kale** or **spinach**

also work well), sliced • 3 ounces Gruyère cheese, grated

Preheat the oven to 400°F. Put the milk, cream, garlic, thyme, and bay leaves in
a saucepan and season. Simmer gently for 3 minutes, then remove from the heat.
Add the turnips, and add more milk to cover if necessary. Simmer until just tender.
Lightly steam the turnip greens until almost tender. Strain the turnips, reserve
the creamy milk, and remove the thyme and bay leaves. Layer the turnips, turnip
greens, and cheese in a 1 quart oval baking dish, pouring the creamy milk over each
layer. Top with the cheese. Bake for 30 minutes, or until golden and bubbling.

HEALING CURRY BOWL

Serves: 4 people — Time: 40 minutes

CONTAINS
Vitamins A, B6, and C, fiber, carotenoids, potassium

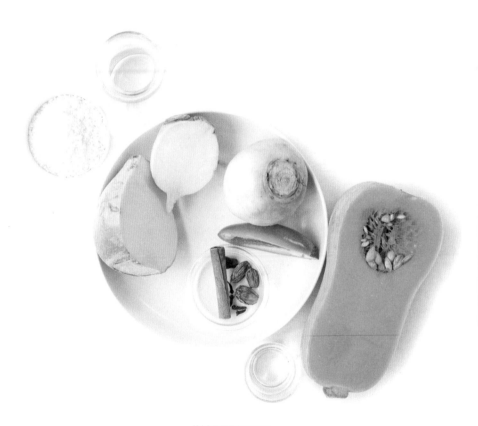

INGREDIENTS

1 ounce desiccated coconut flakes • ½ cup boiling water

3 tablespoons vegetable oil • 4 cardamom pods • 4 cloves

1 medium jalapeño, sliced in half lengthwise and seeded • ½ cinnamon stick

½ butternut **squash** (about 18 ounces), peeled, seeded, and cut into 1-inch pieces

½ medium **rutabaga** (about 9 ounces), peeled and cut into 1-inch pieces

1½ medium **turnips** (about 9 ounces), peeled and cut into 1-inch pieces

¼ teaspoon sea salt flakes

Soak the coconut in the boiling water and set aside. Heat the oil in a large saucepan until very hot, then add the cardamom pods, cloves, chile, and cinnamon stick. Cook for 30 seconds, stirring constantly, then add the vegetables. Cook, stirring, until golden, about 8 minutes. Reduce the heat to low, add the salt, and cook, covered, until the vegetables are very tender, about 20 minutes. Stir often to ensure they don't stick. Add the coconut and water. Stir to coat, and cook for a few minutes more until the water has evaporated before serving.

MEDITERRANEAN VEGETABLE BOWL

Serves: 4 people — Time: 40 minutes

CONTAINS

Vitamins A, B group, C, and K, flavonoids,
carotenoids, folate, fiber

INGREDIENTS

1 small eggplant (about 10 ounces), cut into large cubes • 1 teaspoon fine sea salt

½ cup olive oil • 1 red onion, thinly sliced • 2 cloves garlic, finely chopped

2 large ripe **tomatoes**, diced • ½ **red bell pepper**, seeded and diced

5 ounces **artichoke hearts** in oil (drained weight), cut into bite-sized pieces

1 heaping tablespoon capers • 1 ounce golden raisins

A generous pinch of chile flakes • 2 tablespoons red wine vinegar

Sea salt flakes • Freshly ground black pepper • A handful of **basil**, torn

Place the eggplant in a colander set over a bowl, sprinkle with the salt, and drain
for 20 minutes, then pat dry with paper towels. Heat 2 tablespoons of the oil in
a frying pan and cook the onion until soft, about 8 minutes. Add the garlic and
cook for 2 minutes. Transfer to a plate and wipe out the pan. Heat the remaining
oil over medium-high heat and fry the eggplant until golden. Return the onion
and garlic and add the tomatoes, red pepper, and ½ cup of water. Simmer for
15 minutes. Remove from the heat and add the remaining ingredients. Season
with sea salt flakes and pepper and sprinkle with basil.

ULTIMATE LENTIL BRAISE

Serves: 4 people – Time: 45 minutes

CONTAINS

Vitamins B group and C, flavonoids, carotenoids,
molybdenum, folate, fiber

INGREDIENTS

2 tablespoons olive oil • 2 onions, chopped

3 cloves garlic, finely chopped • 1⅓ cups **Puy lentils**, rinsed and drained

1 (14-ounce) can diced **tomatoes** • 2½ cups vegetable stock

POTENTIAL
BENEFITS

protects against
cardiovascular disease and
cancer • **lowers** *cholesterol*
• **regulates** *blood sugar*
• **supports** *bone health*
and weight loss

Heat the oil in an ovenproof saucepan, or Dutch oven. Add the onions, and cook
over medium heat until they start to soften, about 5 minutes. Add the garlic and
a splash of water, then reduce the heat and cover. Cook for 10 minutes, or until soft,
adding more water if needed. Add the lentils and simmer for a few minutes more.
Add the tomatoes and stock, cover, and cook for 20 to 30 minutes.

SUPERCHARGED CARROTS

Serves 4 people – Time: 30 minutes

CONTAINS

Vitamins A, B7, C, and K, carotenoids, copper,
flavonoids, manganese, calcium

INGREDIENTS

1 large bunch of **carrots** with the green tops on • ½ cup extra-virgin
olive oil, divided • Sea salt flakes • Freshly ground black pepper
2 tablespoons **lemon juice** • 1 clove garlic, crushed • 2 tablespoons honey
¼ teaspoon whole-grain mustard • 1 tablespoon **black sesame seeds**

POTENTIAL
BENEFITS

protects against
*cardiovascular disease,
rheumatoid arthritis, cell damage,
osteoporosis, and cancer*
• **supports** *eye, vascular,
respiratory, and bone health
and the immune system*
• *anti-inflammatory*

Set the oven to 400°F. Cut the green tops off the carrots, coarsely chop,
and set aside. On a baking tray, toss the carrots with 2 tablespoons of olive
oil and season with salt and pepper. Roast for 25 to 30 minutes, or until
tender and starting to caramelize. For the dressing, place the olive oil, lemon
juice, garlic, honey, and mustard in a food processor and blend. Season with
salt and pepper to taste. Add the carrot tops and briefly blend again. When
the carrots are cooked, toss with enough of the dressing to coat, and sprinkle
with sesame seeds. Serve with the rest of the dressing on the side.

POWERHOUSE TOMATOES

Serves 4 people – Time: 1½ hours

CONTAINS
Vitamins B group, C, and K, flavonoids, carotenoids

INGREDIENTS
6 medium **tomatoes**, halved • 3 cloves garlic, crushed • A large handful of **basil**

3 tablespoons olive oil • Sea salt flakes • Freshly ground black pepper

POTENTIAL
BENEFITS

protects against
*cardiovascular disease and
cancer* • **lowers** *cholesterol*
• **regulates** *blood sugar*
• **supports** *bone health and
weight loss* • *antibacterial*

Preheat the oven to 325°F. Place the tomatoes on a baking tray. Mix all the other ingredients together in a screw-top jar, then pour the mixture over the tomatoes and toss them in it. Arrange in the tray cut-side down and roast for 1 to 1½ hours, depending on ripeness and size. They should be very soft and wrinkled when done. Serve hot or cold.

WARM GARDEN SALAD

Serves 4 people — Time: 40 minutes

CONTAINS

Vitamin A, C, and K, carotenoids, folate, flavonoids

INGREDIENTS

2 bunches mild **radishes** with tops on

6 red or green **Belgian endives**, halved lengthwise • 6 tablespoons

unsalted butter, melted • 2 tablespoons olive oil • 2 tablespoons honey

A generous squeeze of **lemon juice** • 1 sprig thyme, leaves removed

Sea salt flakes • Freshly ground black pepper

Preheat the oven to 375°F. Cut the tops off the radishes, trim the leaves, and set
aside. Halve or quarter the radishes so they are roughly the same size and place
on a baking tray with the endive halves. Whisk together the butter, olive oil, honey,
lemon juice, and thyme, and season with salt and pepper. Pour over the vegetables
and toss. Roast for 25 to 30 minutes, until tender, shaking the pan once or twice
during cooking. As soon as the vegetables are cooked, add the radish leaves to the
hot pan, and toss until wilted. Season with salt and pepper to taste, then serve.

HEARTY SPICED STEW

Serves: 2 people — Time: 1½ hours (1 hour active)

CONTAINS
Vitamins A, B group, and C, flavonoids, carotenoids

INGREDIENTS
½ medium eggplant (about 7 ounces), cut into ¾-inch cubes
½ teaspoon fine sea salt • 2 tablespoons olive oil • 3 cloves garlic, chopped
½ red onion, chopped • 1 large **tomato** (about 5 ounces), chopped
1 jalapeño, seeded and finely chopped • ½ teaspoon garam masala
½ **red bell pepper**, stemmed, and chopped into ¾-inch chunks
Sea salt flakes • Freshly ground black pepper

Preheat the oven to 425°F. Place the eggplant in a colander set over a bowl, toss with the salt, and drain for 30 minutes. Pat dry, place on a baking tray lined with parchment paper, and toss with half of the oil. Roast for 15 minutes, or until tender. Heat the remaining oil in a frying pan and sauté the garlic and onion until golden, about 5 minutes. Add the tomatoes, jalapeño, and garam masala and cook for 2 minutes. Stir in the bell pepper, eggplant, 3 tablespoons of water, and salt and pepper to taste. Cover and cook for 30 minutes, or until tender, adding more water if it dries out.

MAIN DISHES

Anyone who believes that highly nutritious main meals must, by definition, be dull and boring should think again. These vibrant plates are absolutely delicious—and also happen to be incredibly beneficial for your health and well-being.

GLOWING GREEN PESTO PASTA

Serves: 1 person – Time: 15 minutes

CONTAINS
Vitamins A, B group, C, and K, manganese,
glucosinolates, flavonoids, copper,

INGREDIENTS
3½ ounces fusilli pasta • 2 tablespoons extra-virgin olive oil, plus more
¾ ounce **kale**, tough stalks removed, chopped • ½ clove garlic
½ cup **basil** leaves • ⅓ cup unsalted **roasted peanuts**, coarsely chopped, plus more
for sprinkling • ½ ounce Parmesan cheese, grated, plus more for sprinkling
Lemon juice • Sea salt flakes • Freshly ground black pepper

Cook the pasta according to the package instructions. Drain and toss with a little olive oil. Meanwhile, scrunch the kale with your hands to soften it, place in a food processor and pulse to a coarse paste. Add the garlic, the 2 tablespoons of olive oil, the basil, peanuts, and Parmesan. Process to the desired consistency, adding more oil if necessary. Add lemon juice, salt, and pepper to taste, then toss with the hot pasta. Serve sprinkled with Parmesan and chopped peanuts.

NOURISHING NOODLE BOWL

Serves: 1 person – Time: 25 minutes

CONTAINS
Vitamins A, B group, C, D, and K, selenium, omega-3
fatty acids, potassium, glucosinolates

INGREDIENTS
1 skinless **salmon fillet**, about 4 ounces • 3 tablespoons soy sauce
3½ ounces medium-wide flat rice noodles • 2 tablespoons peanut
or any other flavorless oil, plus more for tossing • 1 small bunch
bok choy, leaves separated • A pinch of chile flakes

96

POTENTIAL
BENEFITS

protects against
cardiovascular disease and
cancer • **supports** *eye*
and joint health
• anti-inflammatory

Place the salmon in a shallow bowl, pour over half the soy sauce, and turn to coat. Set aside. Meanwhile, soak the noodles in boiling water for 5 minutes, then rinse and toss with a splash of oil. Set aside. Heat 1 tablespoon of the oil in a frying pan and cook the salmon for 2 to 3 minutes on each side, until just cooked through. Flake the fish and set aside. Wipe out the pan, add the remaining oil, and stir-fry the bok choy for 1 minute. Add the noodles, chile flakes, salmon, and remaining soy sauce and gently toss. Serve immediately.

CAULIFLOWER RISOTTO

Serves: 1 person — Time: 20 minutes

CONTAINS

Vitamins C and K, folate, protein, iron, magnesium,
calcium, fiber, flavonoids

INGREDIENTS

10 ounces **cauliflower**, broken into small florets • 1 heaping teaspoon
white miso paste • 1½ tablespoons unsalted butter • 1½ teaspoons olive oil
1 shallot, finely chopped • 3 ounces **artichoke hearts** in oil (drained weight),
cut into bite-size pieces • 3 heaping tablespoons finely grated Parmesan, plus more
Finely grated zest of ½ **lemon** • Sea salt flakes
Freshly ground black pepper • A handful of **basil** leaves, sliced

Pulse the cauliflower in a food processor to the size of rice grains. Dissolve the
miso paste in 1¼ cups boiling water. Heat 1 tablespoon of the butter and the oil in
a pan, add the shallot, and gently cook for 5 minutes, until soft. Add the cauliflower
and stir to coat. Add half the miso stock and simmer for 10 minutes, stirring and
adding a bit more stock now and then. The cauliflower should be tender but retain
some bite, with enough liquid left to make a sauce. Fold in the artichokes, remove
from the heat, and add the remaining butter, the Parmesan, lemon zest, and salt
and pepper to taste. Serve sprinkled with basil and Parmesan.

DETOX BOWL

Serves: 1 person — Time: 40 minutes

CONTAINS

Vitamins A, B group, C, and E, fiber, carotenoids,
flavonoids and other phytochemicals, manganese, copper

INGREDIENTS

½ **acorn squash** (about 10 ounces), peeled, seeded, and cut into bite-size chunks

¼ cup olive oil, plus extra for drizzling • Sea salt flakes

Freshly ground black pepper • 5 ounces giant (Israeli) couscous

1½ cups chicken or vegetable stock • 1 tablespoon **lemon juice**

1 teaspoon Dijon mustard • A handful of arugula

A handful of **dried cranberries** • A handful of **pecans**, chopped

Preheat the oven to 400°F. Place the squash on a baking tray, drizzle with olive oil, and season with salt and pepper. Roast for 20 to 30 minutes, or until tender and slightly caramelized. Place the couscous in a saucepan, add 1 tablespoon of oil, and stir over medium-high heat until toasted. Add the stock, bring to a boil, then reduce the heat to low and cover. Cook for 15 minutes, or until the stock is absorbed. Whisk together the remaining oil, lemon juice, mustard, and salt and pepper to taste in a small bowl. When the couscous is cooked, remove from the heat, add the arugula and stir until wilted. Add the dressing, cranberries, pecans, and squash.

GREEN PASTA BAKE

Serves: 1 person — Time: 1 hour

CONTAINS

Vitamins A, B group, C, E, and K, manganese, folate,
calcium, flavonoids, magnesium, glucosinolates, copper,
carotenoids, selenium, fiber

INGREDIENTS

3 ounces penne pasta • 4 teaspoons unsalted butter, plus more for greasing

2 tablespoons all-purpose flour • 1 cup milk, plus more

1½ ounces Comte, Gruyère, or cheddar cheese, grated • ¼ teaspoon paprika

A pinch of nutmeg • ½ teaspoon Dijon mustard • Sea salt flakes

Freshly ground black pepper • 1½ ounces **collard greens,**

beet greens, turnip greens, kale, or **spinach,** finely sliced

1 ounce sourdough or country-style bread, torn • 2 teaspoons extra-virgin olive oil

2 teaspoons **sunflower seeds** • 2 teaspoons **ground hazelnuts**

Cook the penne in salted boiling water according to the package instructions.
Drain and set aside. Preheat the oven to 350°F and lightly butter a 1 quart
gratin dish. Melt the butter in a pan until foaming, then add the flour. Stir
constantly over medium heat for 1 minute, then gradually whisk in the milk. Gently
cook for 5 minutes until starting to thicken, then stir in the cheese, seasonings,
greens, and pasta. Pour the pasta mixture into the dish. Pulse the bread, oil,
sunflower seeds, and hazelnuts in a food processor until the mixture resembles
bread crumbs. Sprinkle over the pasta and bake for 30 minutes.

COZY ROOT VEGETABLE SALAD

Serves: 1 person — Time: 50 minutes

CONTAINS
Vitamins A, B group, C, and K, carotenoids, flavonoids

INGREDIENTS

2 medium **carrots**, cut lengthwise and crosswise

½ medium **turnip** (about 3 ounces), peeled and cut into 3 by 1-inch batons

3 tablespoons olive oil • 2 tablespoons **lemon juice** • Sea salt flakes

Freshly ground black pepper • 2 ounces **cherry tomatoes**, quartered

1 cup cooked wheat berries or farro • 2 ounces feta cheese, crumbled

POTENTIAL
BENEFITS

protects against
cardiovascular disease,
rheumatoid arthritis, cell damage,
and cancer • **lowers**
cholesterol • **supports** *eye*
and bone health, immune
system, and weight loss
• anti-inflammatory

Preheat the oven to 400°F. Place the carrots and turnips on a baking tray.
Toss with 1 tablespoon of the olive oil and half the lemon juice and season with
salt and pepper. Bake for 20 minutes, add the tomatoes and toss to coat in
the pan juices then roast for a further 20 minutes, or until tender. Toss the wheat
berries, feta cheese, and roasted vegetables with the remaining olive oil and
lemon juice, and add salt and pepper to taste. Serve immediately.

KALE AND BEAN HASH

Serves: 1 person – Time: 20 minutes

CONTAINS
Vitamins A, B group, C, E, and K, manganese,
glucosinolates, flavonoids, copper, fiber, selenium

INGREDIENTS
2 ounces **curly kale**, thick stalks removed, finely sliced

1 tablespoon olive oil, plus more if needed • ½ clove garlic, minced

1 heaping tablespoon coarse bread crumbs, ideally from a rye or sourdough loaf

1 tablespoons **hazelnuts**, finely chopped • 1 tablespoon **sunflower seeds**

Grated zest and juice of ½ **lemon** • A pinch of chile flakes

3 tablespoons parsley, chopped • Sea salt flakes • Freshly ground black pepper

½ cup cooked or canned gigante or Great Northern beans, drained and rinsed

3 tablespoons finely grated Parmesan

Steam the kale until tender. Set aside. Heat half the oil in a frying pan and briefly cook the garlic until pale gold. Add the bread crumbs, hazelnuts, and sunflower seeds, and stir-fry over medium-high heat until crisp. Stir in the lemon zest, chile flakes, and parsley, and season with salt and pepper. Set aside. Wipe out the pan, add the remaining olive oil, and cook the beans in a single layer for a couple of minutes until golden underneath, then flip and cook the other side. Add the kale, gently toss, and stir in the lemon juice. Generously season with salt and pepper. Serve the beans and kale topped with the bread crumb mixture and Parmesan.

BEAN AND CHOCOLATE CHILI

Serves: 1 person — Time: 40 minutes

CONTAINS

Vitamins B group and C, flavonoids, carotenoids,
molybdenum, folate, fiber, minerals, flavonoids

INGREDIENTS

1 tablespoon olive oil • ½ red onion, chopped • 1 small clove garlic, chopped

½ small red chile, such as cayenne, finely sliced • ½ cup **tomato purée**

5 tablespoons vegetable stock, plus more if needed • Scant cup canned

red kidney beans, rinsed and drained • ⅓ ounce unsweetened **chocolate**

(100% cacao), shaved • ½ teaspoon ground cumin • Sea salt flakes

Freshly ground black pepper • A squeeze of lime

Heat the oil in a small pan and gently sauté the onion until soft, about
8 minutes. Add the garlic and chile, and cook for a few minutes more. Add
the tomato purée, stock, beans, chocolate, and cumin, and season with salt
and pepper. Bring to a boil, reduce the heat, and gently simmer, uncovered,
for 20 minutes, stirring regularly. Add the lime juice and more salt and
pepper to taste. This dish is delicious served with steamed rice.

ROASTED MACKEREL AND SALSA

Serves: 1 person — Time: 20 minutes

CONTAINS

Vitamins B group, C, D, and K, omega-3 fatty acids,
flavonoids and other phytochemicals, carotenoids

INGREDIENTS

1 whole **mackerel**, cleaned and gutted • 2 slices of **lemon**, plus the juice
of ½ lemon • Sea salt flakes • Freshly ground black pepper
5 **cherry tomatoes**, 3 halved and 2 diced • 2 tablespoons olive oil, plus more for
drizzling • ½ clove garlic, finely chopped • 1 tablespoon chopped **cilantro**

Preheat the oven to 350°F. Cut 3 slashes in both sides of the mackerel. Stuff the inside with the lemon slices and season inside and out with salt and pepper. Place in a small baking dish and pour over the lemon juice. Arrange the halved tomatoes around the fish and drizzle with olive oil. Bake for 15 minutes, or until the flesh comes away from the bone easily. Heat the 2 tablespoons of olive oil in a small pan over low heat, add the garlic, and gently cook about 2 minutes. Add the diced tomatoes and cilantro and warm through. Serve the fish with the sauce spooned over and the diced tomatoes alongside.

MACKEREL AND SUPERSAUCE TOAST

Serves: 1 person — Time: 20 minutes

CONTAINS
Vitamins B group, C, and D, omega-3 fatty acids,
flavonoids, carotenoids

INGREDIENTS

1 **mackerel** fillet • 1 tablespoon olive oil, plus more for brushing

½ teaspoon fine sea salt • ½ red onion, finely chopped

1½ teaspoons balsamic vinegar • ½ cup **tomato purée** • ¼ teaspoon smoked paprika

Sea salt flakes • Freshly ground black pepper • 1 slice sourghdough bread

Brush both sides of the mackerel with oil and sprinkle with the fine sea salt. Heat
1 tablespoon oil in a small pan, add the onion, and cook until soft, about 8 minutes.
Add the vinegar and cook until reduced to a syrup, about 5 minutes. Stir in the
tomato purée, paprika, ¼ cup of water, and salt and pepper to taste. Gently simmer
until reduced to a thick sauce, about 10 minutes, then remove from the heat.
Put the mackerel on a foil-lined tray skin-side up and cook under the broiler for
2 minutes, or until the skin bubbles. Flip and grill for 1 minute. Toast the bread.
To serve, place the mackerel on the toast with the sauce spooned over.

SALMON WITH WATERCRESS SAUCE

Serves: 1 person — Time: 20 minutes

CONTAINS

Vitamins A, B group, C, D, and K, selenium, omega-3
fatty acids, flavonoids

INGREDIENTS

1 **salmon fillet**, about 4 ounces • A squeeze of **lemon** • Sea salt flakes
Freshly ground black pepper • 1 tablespoon unsalted butter
1 shallot, finely chopped • 2 ounces **watercress**
¼ cup chicken, fish, or vegetable stock • 1 tablespoon crème fraîche

Preheat the oven to 350°F. Place the salmon in a baking dish, squeeze over
the lemon, and season with salt and pepper. Cover tightly with foil and roast for
15 minutes. Melt the butter in a pan and cook the shallot until soft, about 4 minutes.
Chop half the watercress (including stalks) and add. Stir-fry for 2 minutes, then add
the stock. Cook for 1 minute, stir in the crème fraîche, and season with salt and
pepper. Cool slightly, purée in a blender until smooth, then pass through a
fine-mesh sieve if desired. Add salt and pepper to taste before warming through.
Remove the tough stalks from the remaining watercress and place the leaves
on a plate. Top with the salmon and sauce.

SALMON BURGER

Serves: 1 person — Time: 45 minutes (25 active)

CONTAINS

Vitamins A, B group, C, D, and K, folate, carotenoids,
selenium, omega-3 fatty acids

INGREDIENTS

1 skinless **salmon fillet**, about 4 ounces, cut into pieces

½ teaspoon fresh grated ginger • ½ clove garlic, minced

¼ cup fresh bread crumbs • Sea salt flakes • Freshly ground black pepper

All-purpose flour, for dusting • 2 tablespoons canola or peanut oil

Burger bun • 1 tablespoon mayonnaise • A handful of **arugula**, to serve

POTENTIAL
BENEFITS

protects against
*cardiovascular disease
and cancer*
• **supports** *joint and
eye health*

Pulse the salmon in a food processor until coarsely chopped. Transfer to a bowl
and mix in the ginger, garlic, and bread crumbs. Season with salt and pepper
to taste. Shape into a patty and chill for 20 minutes. Then lightly dust the salmon
patty with flour. Heat the oil in a frying pan and fry the patty for 3 to 4 minutes
on each side. Serve in a burger bun on top of mayonnaise and arugula.

CHEESY VEGETABLE PIE

Serves: 1 person — Time: 1 hour

CONTAINS

Vitamins A, C, and K, manganese,
glucosinolates, flavonoids

INGREDIENTS

2 teaspoons olive oil • ¼ yellow onion, finely diced • 2 to 3 purple or new potatoes
(about 3 ounces), diced • 3 to 4 baby **turnips** (about 3 ounces), diced
Sea salt flakes • Freshly ground black pepper • ¾ ounce **kale**, stems removed,
finely shredded • 1 (8-inch) square sheet puff pastry, 1¼ inch thick
2 ounces cheddar cheese, grated

Heat the oil in the pan and sauté the onion until softened, about 4 minutes. Add the diced potatoes and turnips and fry until softened, another 10 to 15 minutes. Season with salt and pepper and add the kale. Mix to combine, cook for 1 to 2 minutes, reduce the heat to low, cover, and cook for 20 minutes, until just tender. Preheat the oven to 425°F. Place the pastry on a baking sheet lined with parchment paper. Mix the cheese into the vegetables, then spoon onto the lower half of the pastry, leaving a ⅓-inch border. Brush the border with water, fold the pastry over, and press the edges together. Cut slits in the top, then bake for 25 minutes until golden.

BAKED GOODIES

*These sweet and savory breads, cakes,
and baked snacks are a pretty tasty way to
take your vitamins and nutrients. Children,
who sometimes shy away from the good stuff,
seem to have no problem devouring these.*

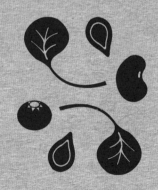

SOFT SEEDY LOAF

Makes: 1 large loaf – Time: 3½ hours (1 hour active)

CONTAINS
Vitamins B group and E, copper, manganese, selenium,
calcium, omega-3 fatty acids, phosphorous, fiber

INGREDIENTS
10 tablespoons **sunflower seeds** • 3⅓ cups bread flour • 1½ teaspoons fine sea salt
2¼ teaspoons fast-acting dry yeast • 2 tablespoons honey mixed with
1⅓ cups warm water • 1 egg, lightly beaten with a splash of water
2 tablespoons mixed seeds, such as **flax**, **chia**, and **sesame seeds**

Pulse the sunflower seeds in a food processor. Whisk together the flour, chopped
seeds, salt, and yeast, then stir in the honey water. Turn out onto an oiled surface
and knead. Set aside in an oiled bowl, covered, for 15 minutes. Knead and set aside
twice more. Leave for 1 hour. Flatten the dough, roll it, and put it seam-side down
in an oiled oval pan. Cover with plastic wrap. Leave for 30 minutes. Preheat the oven
to 400°F. Brush the dough with the egg wash, sprinkle with the seeds, then brush
with more egg. Bake for 40 minutes. Leave for 10 minutes, then cool on a wire rack.

CHEESY SEEDY CRACKERS

Makes: about 18 — Time: 60 minutes (30 minutes active)

CONTAINS

Vitamins B group and E, copper, manganese, selenium,
calcium, omega-3 fatty acids, phosphorous, fiber

INGREDIENTS

4 tablespoons unsalted butter, diced • 4 ounces strong cheddar cheese, grated

½ cup whole wheat flour, plus more for dusting • ½ teaspoon sea salt flakes

Freshly ground black pepper • 2 teaspoons **sesame seeds**

2 teaspoons **sunflower seeds** • 2 teaspoons **chia seeds**

Mix the butter and cheese in a food processor, add the flour and salt and pepper
to taste, then pulse to form a sticky dough. Transfer to a bowl, add the seeds, and
knead to combine. Tip onto a floured surface and shape into a sausage about
2 inches in diameter. Wrap in waxed paper and chill for 30 minutes. Preheat the
oven to 350°F and line a baking sheet with parchment paper. Slice the dough into
⅛-inch discs and place on the sheet, leaving spaces between. Bake for 10 minutes,
or until pale gold. Leave for a few minutes, then cool on a wire rack.

SUPERCHARGED MUFFINS

Makes: 12 muffins – Time: 45 minutes

CONTAINS
Vitamin A, B group, C, E, and K, omega-3 fatty acids,
manganese, calcium, phosphorous, fiber, copper,
selenium, folate, carotenoids, protein, iron, magnesium

INGREDIENTS
3¼ cups self-rising flour • 1 teaspoon baking powder • 1 tablespoon wheat bran

1 heaping teaspoon dried oregano • 1 teaspoon nigella seeds

3 tablespoons mixed seeds, such as **chia**, **flax**, and **sunflower** • Sea salt flakes

Freshly ground black pepper • 3½ ounces **baby spinach**, finely sliced

3½ ounces **red peppers** in oil (drained weight), chopped • 5 ounces feta cheese,

crumbled • 2 tablespoons Parmesan cheese, finely grated, plus extra for sprinkling

1⅓ cups **soy** or dairy milk • 4 tablespoons olive oil • 1 large egg

Preheat the oven to 400°F and line a large 12-hole muffin pan with paper
liners. Whisk together the flour, baking powder, bran, oregano, and seeds,
and season generously with salt and pepper. Add the spinach, peppers, feta, and
Parmesan and stir to combine. Whisk together the milk, oil, and egg. Mix
the wet mixture into the dry mixture until just combined, then spoon into the
prepared liners. Sprinkle with Parmesan and bake for 30 minutes, or until
golden and an inserted skewer comes out clean.

MOIST AND SEEDY RUTABAGA CAKE

Makes: an 8-inch square cake — Time: 1 hour 45 minutes

CONTAINS

Vitamins B group, C, and E, omega-3 fatty acids,
manganese, calcium, phosphorous, fiber, copper,
selenium, potassium, carotenoids, flavonoids

INGREDIENTS

7 tablespoons unsalted butter, plus more for greasing

2 cups self-rising flour • ½ teaspoon ground nutmeg • ½ cup mixed seeds,

such as **chia**, **sunflower**, **flax**, and pumpkin • ½ teaspoon fine sea salt

3 eggs • ½ cup packed light brown sugar • 2 tablespoons maple syrup

⅓ cup Greek yogurt • 7 tablespoons **hazelnut oil** • 2 teaspoons vanilla extract

½ medium **rutabaga** (about 5 ounces), grated

2 cups sifted confectioners' sugar • Grated zest and juice of 1 small **orange**

Preheat the oven to 350°F. Grease an 8-inch square cake pan with butter and line with parchment paper. In a mixing bowl, whisk together the flour, nutmeg, seeds, and salt. In another bowl, beat together the eggs, sugar, maple syrup, yogurt, oil, and vanilla. Stir the wet ingredients into the dry ingredients, then fold in the rutabaga. Pour into the pan and bake for 25 minutes, or until an inserted skewer comes out clean. Leave for 10 minutes then turn out onto a wire rack. Once the cake is completely cool, about 2 hours, beat together the butter, confectioners' sugar, and orange zest and juice until fluffy. Spread over the cooled cake, then cut it into squares.

GUILT-FREE CRUMBLE CAKE

Serves: 8 people – Time: 1 hour 15 minutes

CONTAINS
Vitamins B group, C, and E, copper, manganese,
calcium, selenium, fiber, flavonoids, phytochemicals

INGREDIENTS
1 cup all-purpose flour • 4 tablespoons cold unsalted butter, diced
1 cup plus 2 tablespoons superfine sugar • 3 tablespoons rolled oats
1 tablespoon **sesame seeds** • 1 tablespoon **sunflower seeds** • 2 teaspoons
ground cinnamon • ½ cup unsalted butter, softened • Finely grated zest and
juice of 1 small **orange** • 2 eggs, lightly beaten • ½ cup **ground hazelnuts**
1 teaspoon baking powder • A pinch of fine sea salt
6 to 8 **plums**, seeds removed and halved

Preheat the oven to 350°F and butter a 9-inch springform cake pan. For the
crumble, place ¼ cup of the flour in a bowl and cut in the cold butter. Mix in
¼ cup of the sugar, the oats, seeds, and cinnamon. For the cake, beat together the
softened butter, remaining sugar, and orange zest until fluffy. Gradually beat in
the eggs. Whisk together the remaining flour, hazelnuts, baking powder, and salt.
Stir the dry ingredients into the butter mixture, alternating with the orange juice.
Pour into the springform cake pan and push in the plums, cut side down. Top
with the crumble. Bake for 1 hour, or until an inserted skewer comes out clean.

BERRY BURST TART

Serves: 6 people — Time: 1 hour 20 minutes

CONTAINS
Vitamins B group, C, and E, flavonoids, other
phytochemicals, fiber, manganese, copper, carotenoids

INGREDIENTS
1 sheet puff pastry • 7 tablespoons unsalted butter, diced
1 cup granulated sugar • 3 to 4 small red apples, peeled, cored, and halved
½ cup **pecans** • 1 cup fresh or frozen **cranberries**

**POTENTIAL
BENEFITS**

protects against *urinary
tract infection, cardiovascular
disease, cancer,
infection, and cell damage*
• **lowers** *cholesterol*
• **supports** *healthy skin*
• *anti-inflammatory*

Preheat the oven to 350°F. Cut out a 10-inch circle from the pastry, prick with
a fork, and chill. Melt the butter in an 8-inch ovenproof frying pan, sprinkle over
the sugar, and cook over medium heat for 2 minutes until it starts to dissolve.
Arrange the apples cut-side up in the pan. Cook for 30 minutes, shaking the pan
occasionally, until the caramel is golden. Remove from the heat and fill the gaps
between apples with the pecans and cranberries. Cover with the pastry circle
and tuck in the edges with a spoon. Bake for 30 minutes, or until golden brown.
Set aside for 5 minutes, then invert onto a plate. Serve immediately.

ZESTY CHIA CUPCAKES

Makes: 10 to 12 cupcakes — Time: 1 hour 40 minutes

CONTAINS

Vitamin C, flavonoids, protein, iron, magnesium,
calcium, omega-3 fatty acids, manganese,
phosphorous, fiber

INGREDIENTS

⅔ cup all-purpose flour • ½ teaspoon baking powder

A pinch of fine sea salt • Scant 1 cup unsalted butter, softened

½ cup superfine sugar • 2 large eggs, lightly beaten

Finely grated zest and juice of 1 **lemon**

1½ tablespoons **chia seeds** • 1½ cups confectioners' sugar

1 tablespoon **soy milk** • 1½ teaspoons matcha (green tea) powder

Preheat the oven to 350°F and line a 12-hole cupcake pan with paper liners.
Whisk together the flour, baking powder, and salt. Set aside. Beat together
9 tablespoons butter and the superfine sugar until pale and fluffy. Gradually
beat in the eggs, then add the lemon zest and chia seeds. Stir the flour mixture
into the butter mixture, alternating with the lemon juice, until combined.
Spoon into the paper liners and bake for 20 minutes, or until firm. Leave to
cool on a wire rack. Beat the remaining butter until light and fluffy, then add
the confectioners' sugar, milk, and matcha powder. Once the cupcakes are
completely cool, about 1½ hours, top the cooled cupcakes with the buttercream.

CHOCBERRY CUPCAKES

Makes: 12 cupcakes — Time: 40 minutes

CONTAINS

Vitamins B group, C, and E, protein, iron, magnesium,
calcium, manganese, copper, phytochemicals, fiber,
minerals, flavonoids

INGREDIENTS

¾ cup **soy milk** • 3½ tablespoons vegetable oil • 2 tablespoons **hazelnut oil**

1 large egg • 1 teaspoon vanilla extract • ¾ cup superfine sugar

1¼ cups self-rising flour • ⅓ cup **cocoa powder** • 2 tablespoons **ground hazelnuts**

1 teaspoon baking powder • A pinch of salt • 36 **raspberries**

3 ounces **dark chocolate** (70% cacao), broken into squares

Preheat the oven to 350°F and line a 12-hole muffin pan with paper liners.
In a mixing bowl, whisk together the milk, oils, egg, and vanilla. In a large mixing
bowl, mix together the sugar, flour, cocoa powder, hazelnuts, baking powder,
and salt. Stir the wet ingredients into the dry mixture until just combined. Fill the
paper liners one-third full with batter, then press 3 raspberries and 1 square
of chocolate into each. Spoon the remaining batter on top—the liners should
be roughly two-thirds full. Bake for about 20 minutes, or until firm to touch. Leave
in the pan for 10 minutes, then transfer to a wire rack to cool.

STICKY SQUASH CAKE

Makes: 1 large loaf — Time: 1 hour 25 minutes

CONTAINS
Vitamins A, B group, C, and E, fiber, carotenoids,
copper, manganese, selenium, calcium, protein,
iron magnesium

INGREDIENTS

½ cup unsalted butter, plus more for greasing • Scant ½ cup molasses

Scant ½ cup corn syrup • ½ cup packed muscovado sugar

¼ **acorn squash**, about (5 ounces), roasted and puréed (see page 29)

2 teaspoons fresh ginger, finely grated • 1 large egg, lightly beaten

1⅓ cups self-rising flour • ¼ cup **mixed seeds**, such as **flax**, **sesame**, **pumpkin**,

and **sunflower**, ground to a coarse powder • 1 teaspoon baking soda

1 teaspoon ground ginger • 1 teaspoon ground cinnamon • 1 teaspoon allspice

¾ cup plus 2 tablespoons **soy** or dairy milk

Preheat the oven to 325°F. Butter a large loaf pan and line the bottom with parchment paper. Place the butter, molasses, corn syrup, and sugar in a pan over low heat until the butter has melted. Stir in the squash purée and fresh ginger.

Set aside to cool for 5 minutes, then stir in the egg. In a mixing bowl, whisk together the flour, seeds, baking soda, and spices. Stir the molasses mixture into the flour mixture, then gradually add the milk to make a thin batter. Pour into the pan and bake for 50 minutes, or until an inserted skewer comes out clean. Leave for 10 minutes, then turn out onto a wire rack to cool.

VIRTUOUS BROWNIES

Makes: 16 large squares – Time: 50 minutes

CONTAINS

Vitamins A, B group, C, and E, minerals, flavonoids,
phytochemicals, manganese, copper, fiber

INGREDIENTS

1¾ ounces **dark chocolate** (70% cacao), coarsely chopped

1¾ ounces **skinless hazelnuts**, toasted and coarsely chopped • 1½ ounces **cacao nibs**

10 tablespoons unsalted butter, melted • 1¼ cups superfine sugar

Scant 1 cup **cocoa powder** • A generous pinch of fine sea salt

2 large eggs, lightly beaten • 6½ tablespoons self-rising flour

1 ounce **dried sour cherries**

POTENTIAL
BENEFITS

protects against *cancer*
and cardiovascular disease
• **lowers** *cholesterol*
• **supports** *weight loss and skin*
and nervous system health
• *anti-inflammatory,*
antidepressant, mild
stimulant

Preheat the oven to 325°F. Line an 8-inch square pan with parchment paper, letting the paper hang over the sides. Combine the chocolate, hazelnuts, and cocoa nibs in a bowl. Set aside. Melt the butter in a heatproof bowl over a pan of simmering water. Remove from the heat and beat in the sugar, cocoa powder, and salt. Leave to cool slightly, for 2 to 3 minutes, then beat in the eggs. Stir in the flour and cherries. Put half the batter in the pan, scatter over half the nut mixture, then spread the remaining batter on top. Scatter with the rest of the nut mixture. Bake for 30 minutes, or until firm. Cool, then cut into squares.

SWEET THINGS

Sweet treats that are actually good for you?
It's true. These delicious desserts and snacks
combine the best of both worlds: decadence
and powerhouse seeds, nuts, and fruit.

STICKY ENERGY BARS

Makes: 10 bars — Time: about 2 hours (10 minutes active)

CONTAINS

Vitamins B group, C, and E, manganese, copper,
carotenoids, fiber, calcium, flavonoids, other
phytochemicals, omega-3 fatty acids, phosphorous,
selenium, iron

INGREDIENTS

¾ cup **pecans**, coarsely chopped • 1 cup **peanuts**, coarsely chopped

⅔ cup **sesame seeds** • ½ cup **chia seeds** • ⅔ cup **dried cranberries**

¼ cup **goji berries** • 6 tablespoons honey or agave nectar

2 tablespoons almond butter • 2 tablespoons coconut oil, melted

1 teaspoon vanilla extract • A generous pinch of fine sea salt

Line a square 8-inch baking pan with foil. In a mixing bowl, combine the nuts
and seeds. Add all the remaining ingredients and stir until everything is well
combined and evenly distributed. Pour into the prepared pan, press in firmly, and
evenly with the back of a spoon and chill until set, about 2 hours. Lift the foil out
carefully and cut into squares. Store in the refrigerator for up to 1 week.

GOODNESS BARS

Makes: 1 large bar — Time: about 2 hours (20 minutes active)

CONTAINS
Vitamins B group, C, and E, copper, manganese,
selenium, flavonoids, other phytochemicals,
minerals, fiber

INGREDIENTS
⅔ cup **sunflower seeds** • ¼ cup **dried cranberries**

½ cup confectioners' sugar sifted

2 ounces unsweetened **chocolate** (100% cacao), grated

3½ tablespoons coconut oil • 2 tablespoons heavy cream • 1 teaspoon vanilla extract

Line a baking sheet with parchment paper. In a frying pan set over medium
heat, warm the sunflower seeds until lightly toasted, about 3 minutes. Add the
cranberries and sprinkle over the sugar. Cook, stirring constantly, until the sugar
has melted and the mixture is sticky. Pour the mixture onto the baking sheet
and use a spoon to flatten into a ¼-inch-thick rectangle. Meanwhile, melt the
chocolate and coconut oil in a heatproof bowl over a pan of simmering water.
Remove from the heat, add the cream and vanilla, and stir until thickened
slightly. Pour over the fruit and seed rectangle and gently spread out to cover.
Chill until set, about 2 hours, then break into pieces to serve.

SPICED CITRUS

Serves: 4 people – Time: 20 minutes

CONTAINS
Vitamins B group, C, and E, lycopene, flavonoids, fiber,
manganese, copper, carotenoids

INGREDIENTS
Scant 1 cup Greek yogurt • ½ teaspoon ground cinnamon
1 tablespoon honey • 3 **ruby grapefruit** • 3 large **oranges**
2 tablespoons unsalted butter • 3 tablespoons dark muscovado sugar
1 teaspoon allspice • A handful of **pecans**, toasted and chopped

Mix together the yogurt, cinnamon, and honey and chill until needed. Peel the grapefruit and oranges and cut away the white pith with a sharp knife. Working over a bowl to catch the juice, cut between the membranes to remove the segments. Heat the butter in a frying pan and add the juice from the bowl, the sugar, allspice, and 3 tablespoons of water. Gently simmer, stirring, until the sugar has dissolved and the liquid has reduced to syrup, about 10 minutes. Spoon the fruit into serving bowls and top with the syrup, spiced yogurt, and pecans. Serve immediately.

PLUM AND CRANBERRY CRISP

Serves: 4 people — Time: about 55 minutes

CONTAINS

Vitamins B group, C, and E, copper, manganese,
selenium, calcium, omega-3 fatty acids, phosphorous,
fiber, copper, carotenoids, flavonoids,
other phytochemicals

INGREDIENTS

⅓ cup unsalted butter, chilled and diced, plus more for greasing

⅔ cup whole wheat flour • 3½ tablespoons light brown sugar

2 tablespoons rolled oats • 2 tablespoons **mixed seeds** such as **flax**, **chia**, **sesame**,

and **sunflower** • 2 tablespoons **chopped nuts**, such as **hazelnuts** and **pecans**

a generous pinch of salt • 1 teaspoon ground cinnamon

3 large **plums** (about 14 ounces), quartered • 5 ounces **cranberries**

¼ cup honey • yogurt, crème fraîche, or whipped cream, for serving (optional)

POTENTIAL
BENEFITS
protects against *cancer,
cardiovascular disease, cell
damage, infection, and osteoporosis*
• **lowers** *cholesterol* • **regulates**
blood sugar • **supports** *vascular,
respiratory, digestive, skin, and bone
health, weight loss, iron absorption*
• **eases** *postmenopausal
symptoms* • *anti-
inflammatory*

Preheat the oven to 375°F and lightly butter an 8-inch, 6-cup round baking
dish. To make the crumble, place the flour in a mixing bowl and cut in the
butter until you have small pieces covered in flour. Mix in the sugar, oats, seeds,
nuts, salt, and cinnamon. Chill for 10 minutes. Meanwhile, toss the plums and
cranberries with the honey and place in the prepared dish. Scatter over the
crumble until evenly covered. Bake for 30 minutes, or until golden and bubbling
at the edges. Serve warm with yogurt, crème fraîche, or whipped cream.

SUPER SUNDAE

Serves: 4 people — Time: 15 minutes

CONTAINS
Vitamins A, B group, C, and E, manganese, copper,
fiber, minerals, flavonoids, phytochemicals

INGREDIENTS
⅓ cup skinless **blanched hazelnuts** • ½ teaspoon vanilla extract

1½ ounces fresh dates, pitted • 2 tablespoons **cocoa powder**

A pinch of salt • 6 tablespoons coconut cream, plus more if needed

8 to 12 small scoops vanilla ice cream or frozen yogurt

4 ounces **cherries**, pitted and halved • 2 tablespoons **cacao nibs**

In a frying pan set over medium heat, warm the hazelnuts until lightly toasted, about 3 minutes. Leave to cool a little, then transfer to a food processor and process to a paste. Add the vanilla, dates, cocoa powder, salt, and coconut cream and process until smooth and creamy, adding more coconut cream if necessary to achieve the desired consistency. Distribute the ice cream or frozen yogurt among four glasses or bowls, drizzle over the chocolate sauce, and top with the cherries and cacao nibs.

CHOCOLATE CHIA PUDDING

Serves: 4 people – Time: 10 minutes plus overnight chilling

CONTAINS

Vitamins B group, C, and K, folate, protein,
iron, magnesium, calcium, minerals, flavonoids,
phytochemicals, omega-3 fatty acids, manganese,
phosphorous, fiber

INGREDIENTS

2 cups **soy** or dairy milk • 2 large bananas

2 teaspoons vanilla extract • 2 to 3 tablespoons **cocoa powder**

⅔ cup **chia seeds** • **Raspberries, blueberries**, and **blackberries**, to serve

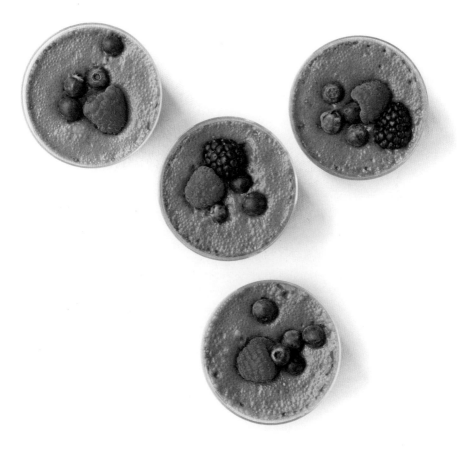

Place the milk, bananas, vanilla, and cocoa powder in a blender and blend until smooth. Transfer to a large bowl and stir in the chia seeds. Cover with plastic wrap and chill overnight. Spoon into bowls and serve topped with berries.

BERRY DREAM FROZEN YOGURT

Serves: 4 people — Time: 20 minutes plus 3 to 4 hours freezing

CONTAINS

Vitamins B group, C, E, and K, folate, manganese,
flavonoids, copper, carotenoids, fiber

INGREDIENTS

1 pound **blackberries** • 1 teaspoon cornstarch

⅓ cup superfine sugar • 2 cups Greek yogurt

¼ cup maple syrup • ½ cup **pecans**, coarsely chopped

POTENTIAL
BENEFITS

protects against *heart
disease, cancer, infection,
and premature aging*
• **lowers** *cholesterol*
• **regulates** *blood sugar*
• **supports** *healthy skin*
• *anti-inflammatory*

Place the blackberries in a saucepan, sprinkle over the cornstarch and sugar, and toss to coat. Mash with a fork, then simmer over medium-high heat, stirring frequently, until completely broken down. Cool for 2 to 3 minutes, then transfer to a food processor and process until smooth. Push through a fine-mesh sieve into a bowl and cool for 5 minutes. Stir in the yogurt, maple syrup, and pecans. Pour into an ice cream maker and freeze according to the manufacturer's instructions. Alternatively, place in a freezer-safe container and freeze for 3 to 4 hours, stirring every hour or so. Blend in a food processor if there are any ice crystals, and serve immediately.

INDEX

Originally published in French in France as *Super Food: La Bible* by Marabout,
a member of Hachette Livre, Paris. This edition was subsequently
published in slightly different form in Australia as *Cooking with Superfoods* by
Hachette Australia, an imprint of Hachette Australia Pty. Limited, Sydney.

Library of Congress Cataloging-in-Publication Data
is on file with the publisher.

Trade Paperback ISBN: 978-1-60774-940-0
eBook ISBN: 978-1-60774-941-7

Printed in China

Photography by Victoria Wall Harris
Food styling by Amelia Wasiliev
Design and illustration by Alice Chadwick

10 9 8 7 6 5 4 3 2 1

First American Edition